HAI R

D0115780

SOCIAL SCIENCE DIVISION
CHICAGO PUBLIC LIBRARY
400 SOUTH STATE STREET
CHICAGO, IL 60605

ENDSHEETS: *Following the custom of the day, the frigate* United States *set the flags of all the countries in the world at her launching in the Delaware River in 1797.*

Broad Stripes
and Bright Stars

Broad Stripe

nd Bright Stars

by Allegheny Trails Council,

Boy Scouts of America,

with headquarters at Flag Plaza,

Pittsburgh, Pennsylvania

American Heritage Press • New York

Grateful acknowledgment is hereby made to
Dr. Whitney Smith, to
The Flag Research Center, Lexington, Massachusetts,
and to
Flag Plaza Foundation, Pittsburgh, Pennsylvania,
for their assistance in
the preparation of this book.

PICTURE CREDITS

Endsheets Courtesy of Mr. Warren Sturgis. **Jacket and Title Page** Courtesy of the White House; photo, Herbert Loebel. **10** Museo del Ejercito, Madrid; photo, Oronoz. **15** National Maritime Museum, Greenwich. **16** Universitatsbibliothek, Heidelberg; Cod. Pal. Germ. 848. **18–19** New-York Historical Society. **23** New York Public Library. **26** Pilgrim Hall. **34** Library of Congress. **38** Seventh Regiment Armory, New York. **40** The Worshipful Society of Apothecaries of London. **46–47** National Gallery of Art, Washington, D.C.; gift of Edgar William and Bernice Chrysler Garbisch. **57** Collection of Alexander McCook Craighead. **58** U.S. Marine Corps. **59** New-York Historical Society. Illustrations appearing on pages **12, 16, 20, 22, 25, 26, 28, 29, 30, 31, 33, 35, 43, 50, 51, 52, 54, 55, 56, 60** were done by Donald Hewitt.

Copyright © 1970 by Flag Plaza Foundation
  and American Heritage Publishing Co., Inc.
All rights reserved.
Published in Canada by Fitzhenry & Whiteside.

SBN: 8281-5010-0 (trade)
      8281-8023-7 (library)

Library of Congress Catalogue Card Number: 73-95742

THE CHICAGO PUBLIC LIBRARY
SEP 28 '70 B

50c

R00214 2736f

TABLE OF CONTENTS

I. NEW NATION, NEW BANNERS

The Flag Salute

On November 16, 1776, the brigantine *Andrew Doria* sailed into harbor at the Dutch West Indian island of St. Eustatius. She was one of the few warships then commissioned by the four-month-old United States, and she was on a special mission. Besides buying gunpowder and other provisions, the *Doria's* captain, Isaiah Robinson, formally delivered to the Dutch governor, Johannes de Graaff, a copy of the Declaration of Independence.

As Christer Greathead, governor of the neighboring British islands of St. Kitts and Nevis, described it, the *Doria* "dropped anchor in the roads of St. Eustatius, and with hoisted flag, known to be that of the rebels called Continental Congress, did . . . salute with thirteen shots the fortress of her high and mighty the Dutch government, called the Orange fort; . . . this salute was afterward answered by that fort with the same solemnity due to the flags of independent sovereign states."

Greathead was already irritated that the authorities at St. Eustatius should permit the trade in gunpowder and other military supplies with the American revolutionaries. The flag salute was the last straw. On December 17, he wrote to De Graaff demanding an explanation "for the offence done to His Majesty's flag by the honor rendered [the American colors] . . . till now unknown in the catalogue of national flags." When he failed to receive a satisfactory reply, he wrote to London, and a direct protest was made to the Dutch government. In response, the flag salute was disavowed, and De Graaff recalled.

The First Flags

Why did the Americans want their flag saluted? Why should the British and Dutch take the salute so seriously? The answer lies in the history and meaning of flags, a rich tradition older than the ancient civilizations of Egypt, India, and China. Primitive man, confronted by a world he

The royal arms of Spain adorned the banner of Francisco Pizarro, Peru's conqueror.

The Vikings may have carried a banner like this when they explored the New World.

did not fully understand, took comfort in symbols. He believed he could influence powerful forces like lightning and fire by drawing pictures of them. He thought that wearing the skin of a wild animal would give him some of the animal's strength, and he looked on familiar objects as friends and protectors. In this way the first flaglike objects. (technically called protovexilloids) were born.

A family or a tribe went into battle bearing its banner at the top of a pole, hoping thus to give courage to the warriors and frighten the enemy. Flags carried in victorious battles or flags handed down from generation to generation became holy objects. The Viking banner is a good example of a flag endowed with mystical powers. The warlike Vikings chose the symbol of the raven, since ravens gathered to feast off the enemies slain on a battlefield. The Danish Vikings who invaded England in the ninth century carried a white flag with the picture of a raven on it. This is how it is described in the *Life of King Aelfred*: "It was a Banner with the Image of a Raven magically wrought by the three Sisters of Hinguar and Hubba . . . made, they say, almost in an instant. . . . It is pretended that being carried in Battle, toward good Success it would always seem to clap the Wings, and do as if it would fly, but toward the Approach of Mishap it would hang right down and not move."

It is even possible that the Vikings carried the raven-flag when they sailed to the New World in the tenth and eleventh centuries.

As man learned more about his environment, he did not abandon his symbols; in fact, they became even more important. In ancient Egypt boats from the different provinces were identified by carved figures of animals mounted on special poles. Boundary stones and battle monuments had to be marked with symbols so that they could be interpreted by everyone, including the majority of the people who were unable to read. In Rome and other empires rulers were able to stay in power partly because their symbols and flags raised them above ordinary men and helped them justify their actions. The kings of León in Spain took the figure of a lion as their special emblem to suggest their bravery, strength, and majesty. The eagle that served as the imperial emblem of the Caesars was adopted by various later empires (Russia, Germany, Austria, France under Napoleon) that claimed in some way to be successors to the Romans. The American use of the eagle as a national bird is at least indirectly based on this tradition.

Skillfully used by dictators or rabble-rousers, symbols can play on the passions of many people. Hitler well understood the technique of coercing with symbols. Although many of his early followers were social misfits, their personalities changed when they put on a uniform and carried the swastika-flag. In their own eyes, and in the eyes of others, their human weaknesses were hidden. They became part of a group—the Nazi party or the "master race"—and their symbols were like magical suits of armor that would protect them against all threats. People were hypnotized and terrorized by the sight of precision marchers bearing thousands of massed banners.

Part of our response to symbols is based simply on habit. There is nothing in the uniform of a policeman or the costume of a nun to make us respect or reject them on first sight. Such responses come from training and experience. For this reason many Americans believe it is very important that adults be required to respect the flag of the United States and that all schoolchildren be asked to recite a pledge of allegiance to it.

The Meaning of the Flag

Flags have always been used to mark special events, to commemorate battles, to honor great men, and to claim rights. When the blacksmith Kave led a revolt against the rulers of Persia, he raised his leather apron as a banner. When Genghis Khan began his conquest of half the world, he announced his intention by hoisting a great white standard fringed with yak tails. During the Middle Ages the sign that a king or emperor had God's approval was his possession of a flag given to him by the pope. William the Conqueror obtained such a flag before he invaded England in the eleventh century; previously, Charlemagne and the Crusaders had carried papal flags. On his first trip to America Columbus carried a special flag given to him by the king and queen of Spain.

In a modern country the flag is flown in countless situations, both ordinary and extraordinary. When the President of the United States speaks to the nation, the national flag and the Presidential color[1] stand behind him. Courts, post offices, and other government offices, military camps, war and merchant ships, schools, and paraders display the flag. Some countries restrict the use of the flag, but in the United States it flies freely over office buildings and homes.

A nation's independence is the most important event marked by the raising of a flag. Since World War II people in dozens of countries in Asia, Africa, and the Pacific have witnessed the dramatic moment when the flag of a colonial power is lowered for the last time. Then a new flag is hoisted on the pole, proclaiming the birth of a new nation to the world. Ships sailing at sea under this flag will not be considered pirates; soldiers and diplomatic representatives of the country will enjoy rights under the protection of the flag; at the United Nations the

Flags proclaim each ship's allegiance as the English defeat the Spanish in 1588.

[1] A "color" is a personal flag.

The French fleur-de-lis as it appeared
during the French and Indian wars

This thirteenth-century knight selected
the fish as his identifying symbol.

flag will assert the equality of the country with all others.

New flags are sometimes conceived during rebellion or civil war. The revolutionaries in France in 1789, in Germany in 1848, in Russia in 1917, and in China in 1949 all felt the need to adopt a new flag to show that the nation had undergone a great change. As we shall see later, the flags of the United States, Texas, and the Confederacy were also born in rebellion. In each case it was a number of years before many countries were willing to recognize the new flag and the government it stood for. The United States, for example, still does not recognize the flag or the government of Communist China.

The Americans were so pleased with the Dutch salute to their flag at St. Eustatius, and the British were so angered by it, because it meant that the rebels would enjoy the military and commercial privileges of an independent state. Even more important, the nations recognizing the flag acknowledged the legal right of the United States to exist.

By the late 1770's Americans were more than just Englishmen living in the New World: they were members of a new and separate nation. At first neither the British *nor* the Americans recognized this fact, as the flags of the era show. Even when independence was finally achieved and The Stars and Stripes received full honors, it was not clear what the personality of the United States would be. How the nation was born, and how it grew, as reflected in its flags, are the stories told in the rest of this book.

Heraldic Banners

Today when a person travels abroad, both he and the nations he visits identify themselves with national symbols. The businessman presents his passport (usually bearing the national coat of arms) to guards who work under their national flag. The car stopping at the colored pole marking a border displays a distinctive license plate. And soldiers have many insignia that distinguish the army to which they belong.

Eight centuries ago, when Europeans in large numbers began to turn their attention to the world around them, national flags had not yet been invented. Heraldic emblems such as shields, crests, and badges came first, and the stories of their origins are as numerous as they are fascinating. Austria, for example, flies a banner of red-white-red horizontal stripes that is supposed to have originated with Duke Leopold V of Babenberg. At the Battle of Acre in 1190 he lost his banner while fighting the Saracens. Having no standard with which to rally his men, he removed the surcoat that covered his armor and hoisted it on a pole as a flag. Since the coat was covered with blood except where it had been belted, it appeared as stripes of red, white, and red. In Spain the arms of Aragon are said to have been improvised by the king when he visited a wounded knight. Touched by the man's loyalty and valor, the king dipped his fingers in the dying soldier's blood and drew them down his own yellow shield. Since then the shield of Aragon has been four red stripes on a yellow background. The three fleurs-de-lis in the arms of France are said to have been toads until the night in A.D. 496 when King Clovis I dreamed of fleurs-de-lis and changed his banner.

These and other tales have been passed down for centuries, but unfortunately most of them are either untrue or highly doubtful. The first coats of arms were adopted for the practical purpose of identification, and the early knights and nobles usually just selected a common object or geometric design for their shield. King Richard I (the

17

When an unknown artist rendered New York harbor about 1757, ten ships were in.

Lion-Hearted) of England chose a lion for his seal, probably to emphasize his courage and strength. The kingdom of Castile in Spain assumed arms that illustrated its name—a castle. In the nineteenth century the American states continued the tradition of including familiar objects in their seals and flags: Louisiana chose the pelican as its symbol; California, the grizzly bear; Maine, the pine tree and the North Star. In both Europe and America, however, coats of arms tended to get more and more complicated with time, as symbols were added to represent new chapters in the territory's history.

Over the years the types and designs of flags used by Europeans

Nine of them were British, and the one at the far left was a captured French ship.

were strongly influenced by the hereditary shields and similar emblems that we call heraldry. Heraldry grew into an art with its own special rules, traditions, and scholars. Even today heraldic language is frequently used to describe a coat of arms.[2] But heraldry depended largely

---

2 Here is a sample of heraldic blazon; it describes the arms appearing on the flag on p. 30: "Azure a round knot of three interlacings and thirteen double foliated ends wavy bellied or; for the crest a horse's head erased proper ensigned with a mullet argent, bitted and rosetted of the second and bridled of the first; for the supporters, dexter, an Indian proper in his dexter hand a Liberty Cap on a pole and in his sinister hand a bow, sinister, an angel blowing on a trumpet held in his dexter hand and holding a rod in his sinister hand, all proper; and for the motto, For These We Strive."

The British cross of St. George　　　　　*The British Union Flag of 1606*

on the kind of rigid social structure found in the feudal system of the Middle Ages. In a modern democratic society, family coats of arms are little more than status symbols. Flags, on the other hand, have become more and more important with the rise of nationalism. And because so few flags today are really heraldic, vexillology, the study of the history and symbolism of flags, has become a separate field. Hobbyists and scholars alike, however, will always be interested in and indebted to the rich heraldic banners of the past.

Bearers of the Cross

Many heraldic flags found their ways to America with the explorers who acted in the name of their king. Columbus and later Spanish explorers hoisted variations of the castles-and-lions banner of the Catholic kings of Spain, while the fleurs-de-lis of France were carried by Cartier, La Salle, La Verendrye, and other Frenchmen on their visits to the New World. One popular European type of flag showed the whole coat of arms on a white field. These are the flags we would see if we could visit the tiny ships anchored in American harbors in the sixteenth and seventeenth centuries, or if we could visit the forts at places like Pittsburgh (Fort Duquesne) ·or New Orleans.

Even in the colonial period other kinds of flags would have caught our eye on a visit to America. Many ships, especially those of Britain and France, flew flags with crosses. Like the flags showing a coat of arms, these crossed flags go back to the Crusades. The rules of heraldry in most European countries restricted the use of arms to kings, nobles, and high church officials. The common soldier in those days had no personal shield or emblem, but he did have a patron saint whom he looked to for protection. The Crusaders ("bearers of the cross") wore the cross of their special saint on their sleeve or surcoat. In time these became national symbols and were used as flags.

In 1385, when the Scots and the French planned an attack on the English, it was required that "every man French and Scots shall have a sign before and behind, namely a white St. Andrew's Cross." (St. Andrew's cross was diagonal, while most other crosses were made from one vertical and one horizontal line.) Thirty-four years later, when King Henry V of England was fighting the French, he ordered his soldiers to identify themselves by decreeing: "every man of what[ever] estate, condition or nacion that he be, of oure partie, bere a band of Seint George suffisant large, upon the perile, if he be wounded or dede in the fawte thereof [i.e., without such a mark], he that hym wounded or sleeth shall bear no peyn for hym." St. George's cross consisted of a red cross on a white background. The French wore a white cross of the same design on a blue background.

In 1606 an event occurred that, as we shall see, was important in the development of the Continental Colors, the first national flag of the United States. King James VI of Scotland had become King James I of England. To show that his rule extended over both parts of Britain, the king created a "Union Flag" by combining England's red cross of St. George and Scotland's white diagonal cross of St. Andrew. English ships, like the *Mayflower* and the ships that sailed to Jamestown, flew the Union Flag along with the plain St. George's cross. The Scots were supposed to display the Union Flag together with St. Andrew's cross, but many of them objected. They found the Union Flag "very prejudicial to the fredome and dignitie of this Estate" because the English cross was placed on top of the Scottish cross. The flag would, they warned, "breid some heit and miscontentment betwix your Majesteis subjectis, and it is to be feirit that some inconvenientis sall fall oute betwix thame." In their letter of complaint to the king they enclosed two Union Flags of their own design, in which Scotland and England were equally represented. "And sua, most humelie beseiking your Majestie [they concluded], as your Heynes has evir had a speciall regaird of the honour, fredome, and libertie of this your Heynes antient and native kingdome that it wuld pleis your sacres Majestie in this particulir to gif unto your Heynes subjectis some satisfactioun and contentment, we pray God to blisse your sacred Majestie with a lang and prosperous reignne and eternall felicitie." But the Union Flag remained unchanged.

In addition to the royal flags with their coats of arms and the national flags with crosses, a few early explorers of America displayed

The Dutch East India Company flag, 1609

the flags of trading and settlement companies. When he sailed up the Hudson River, Henry Hudson flew the orange-white-blue flag of the Netherlands, which honored Prince William of Orange. In the center of that flag was the monogram of the Dutch East India Company, which had sponsored his trip. On the other side of the continent Russian explorers used the white-blue-red flag that Peter the Great had patterned after the Dutch tricolor. The Russian-American Company flag, which flew over forts from Alaska to San Francisco, added the imperial eagle to the national tricolor. Later, in the eighteenth century, both France and Spain adopted striped flags that flew for a while in their American colonies. The Spanish flag adopted in 1785 had red-yellow-red horizontal stripes, and the famous French tricolor of 1794 had blue-white-red vertical stripes. The striped flags of the Netherlands, France, and Spain and the British Union Flag (or Union Jack) still serve today, almost unchanged, as national flags.

Generally speaking, these were the flags that flew in North America for the nearly three hundred years from the time that Columbus landed until the independence of the United States. Like the men who brought them, these flags were essentially European. Little by little, however, the permanent settlers in America felt the urge to have flags and symbols of their own. When officials in the distant mother country failed to provide them, the colonists took matters into their own hands.

Good Men's Zeal

As a Puritan, Captain John Endecott had been taught that church decorations, fancy dress, and similar things were an abomination in the eyes of God. The Massachusetts Bay Colony in which he lived was harsh in this respect; it even outlawed the festive observance of Christmas. But some ministers were stricter in their Puritanism than others, and pastor Roger Williams of Salem was one of the most unbending. He had even said that the cross of St. George in the English flag was a popish idol, a superstitious thing, a relic of the Antichrist. If this were true, Captain Endecott thought to himself, surely it was not right to go into battle carrying a flag that displayed the cross. So one October day in 1634 Endecott strode up to the house of his company's ensign-bearer, Richard Davenport, took the flag, and cut out the red cross. It was not the British Union Jack, or the plain St. George's cross, but a military flag with a solid field of red and a red St. George's cross in the white canton, or upper corner near the pole. So when he had cut out the cross, Endecott was left with a red flag having a blank white square at the top.

The town of Salem was barely eight years old at the time, and in the small close-knit colony news spread fast. On November 5 Richard Brown of nearby Watertown complained to the local government council that Endecott had defaced the flag. The councilmen didn't like the cross, but at the same time they feared the consequences of Endecott's deed. What would happen if news of it should reach England? They decided to pass on this important question to the General Court (or legislature) of the colony, due to meet the following spring. In May, 1635, a special committee considered the problem, then condemned Endecott for his "rashness, uncharitableness, indiscrecon, & exceeding the lymitts of his calling" and made him ineligible to hold any public office for one year. This was a rather serious punishment not only for him but for the community, which had a very small population in

Early English ships entering American ports flew the cross of St. George.

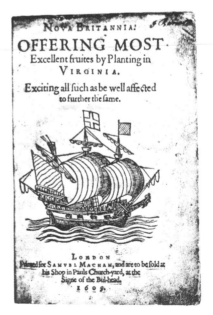

1635. Endecott's standing in the colony is evident from the fact that before and after the flag incident he served for fifteen years as deputy, or assistant, governor of Massachusetts Bay and for thirteen years as its governor.

Endecott had been taken care of, but the problem of the flag remained. Many settlers now argued that the cross should be cut from all their flags. Early in 1636 the military commissioners agreed. This was done; but just when it appeared that everyone was at last satisfied, a British ship entered Boston harbor, and the captain complained. Where, he wanted to know, were the king's colors that should be flying over Fort Independence on Castle Island? Was this a sign that the colonists were in rebellion against the king? The governor hastily called a conference, and after some heated discussion, ordered that the flag with the cross was to be flown whenever ships passed. To satisfy those who objected to the cross, it was made clear that the fort was the king's property, not the colony's, and that the flag flown there was his, not theirs.

The debate about the flag raged for fifty years. Pamphlets and letters were written on both sides, showing why it was (or was not) right to keep the cross. Some feared the wrath of God; others feared punishment by the king; and still others feared the consequences of sailing under an unrecognized flag. There were sermons and debates in the General Court and even sharp words between those companies of local troops that did, and those that did not, show the cross on their flag. In 1643 Massachusetts soldiers in Rhode Island, provoked by the sight of the flag with the cross, shot it down. The king's cross and peace were both finally restored only after 1686, the year in which the New England colonies lost their self-governing powers to a royal governor sent from England. Colonial historian William Hubbard summed up the Endecott incident and the problems it caused: "Good men's zeal doth many times boil over."

Early Colonial Flags

Under the Tudors the British naval flag often had red and white stripes, but in the seventeenth century British merchant ships and men-of-war began to fly ensigns with a plain background—usually red, but sometimes white or blue—with the crossed canton. These appeared not only on the sterns of ships but as company colors for infantry regiments on land. They were familiar, therefore, to Britons both in the mother country and in America. The Red Ensign is especially important because it was the flag that seems to have been the direct ancestor of the first United States flag.

Until 1707 the Red Ensign officially had a solid field of red and a red cross on a white canton. Unofficially, as we have seen, the Massachusetts Bay colonists used a red flag with a plain white canton from 1634 to 1686. Perhaps because they had had their own distinctive flag for so long, the New Englanders were never content simply to go back to the English banner. After 1686, therefore, they created another unofficial flag of their own that they flew on land and probably on their ships. When the St. George's cross was restored to the Red Ensign, New Englanders added a green pine tree in the uppermost corner. And just as the English continued to use the plain St. George's cross (without a red field) as a jack for the prows of their ships, so the jack form of the New England flag was the St. George's cross with a pine tree in the corner.

In 1707, when England and Scotland were abolished as separate kingdoms, the Union Jack replaced the separate crosses of St. George and St. Andrew. This posed a problem for the New Englanders, since the Union Jack (unlike the St. George's cross) had no room on it for a pine tree. Instead of using the Union Jack, therefore, they simply put the tree in the white canton of the Red Ensign. And the new jack had no English or British symbols on it at all. It was just a green tree on a white field, although at times during the Revolution the motto "Appeal to Heaven" was added. What started as a distinction made purely

A fleet of schooners outfitted in 1775 by George Washington flew this banner.

This is a copy of the seal used by the pilgrims who landed at Plymouth Colony.

A Rhode Island revolutionary regiment bore the state's anchor on its flag.

for religious reasons had evolved into a distinctively American flag. In its ensign form one version of the New England flag flew at the Battle of Bunker Hill. In its jack form the design was officially selected in April, 1776, as the flag of the Massachusetts navy. (In fact, this pine-tree flag still flies from the *U.S.S. Massachusetts.*)

Among the early colonies only Maryland had a flag of its own. Maryland was for a long time a proprietary colony, governed by an individual almost as a private principality, rather than by a royal governor or a trading company. The flag of the proprietors (the Lords Baltimore) was used as the flag of Maryland. This black and gold heraldic banner has been modified in modern times to create flags for the State of Maryland, the County of Baltimore, and the City of Baltimore.

If the other colonies did not have this kind of flag, some of them did have distinctive symbols. The pine tree, an important source of income, appeared on many coins. Other familiar things such as the codfish, an Indian, and a ship appeared on official seals, and in newspapers, pamphlets, posters, and handbills different emblems were used to distinguish one colony from another. In the expedition against the French fort of Louisbourg in 1745 colonial troops were identified by pennants—a blue circle on white for Massachusetts and a white circle on blue for Connecticut, Rhode Island, and New Hampshire. Some of these troops also carried a flag picturing a seated Britannia with her shield and a ship.

Coats of arms were granted to some colonies by the king; other colonies invented their own. Connecticut's coat of arms, for example, had fifteen grapevines below a cloud from which the hand of God extended. This suggested their motto: "Qui Transtulit Sustinet," which means, "He Who Brought Us Over Here Will Sustain Us." Later the fifteen vines were reduced to three, probably referring either to the three original towns or to the three colonies that formed Connecticut. A red flag with this coat of arms was used by the state militia during the Revolution. The modern state flag is almost the same, except that the background is blue. In Rhode Island the anchor has been used as a state symbol ever since 1647. The sun in the coat of arms of the State of New York is said to have come from the arms of Jonas Bronck, the first settler in what was then called "the Bronck's land." (Today it is simply known as "the Bronx.") William Penn, the proprietor of what became Pennsylvania, used his personal seal for official papers. Today Delaware, Pennsylvania, and many counties and cities have seals and coats of arms based on Penn's seal.

The Embattled Farmers

On a crisp April morning in 1775 Nathaniel Page, from Bedford, Massachusetts, joined other farmers and craftsmen at the North Bridge to prevent the British from seizing their secret cache of arms in Concord. The American Revolution had begun.

Did Nathaniel Page encourage the men by bringing along the flag that was in his upstairs closet—the flag that showed an armored hand holding a dagger and a ribbon with the Latin inscription "Vince aut Morire" ("Conquer or Die")? We cannot prove it, but it seems very likely. It is possible, too, that the tradition is correct that tells us Page laid the flag aside after the battle so that he could help the men. When he returned, he found a group of boys playing soldier with the banner that had witnessed a momentous turning point in world events. Today that same flag can be seen in the Bedford Town Library.

To have served in such a battle would be distinction enough for any flag, but the "Bedford Flag" may have flown in many battles before that one. It closely resembles the richly made flags that were carried by cavalry troops in the English Civil War of 1642–49, when the Puritans opposed the king. These banners were known as cornets, and they were usually two-and-a-half-foot squares of silk, fringed and

The minutemen carried the Bedford flag at the Battle of Concord in April, 1775.

mounted on a pole. The painted design varied from one troop to another. The infantry carried simpler banners, usually made of linen. The Bedford flag is silk, and it is the right size, which strongly suggests that it was used by cavalry and not infantry and that it was made about one hundred years before the Revolution. A manuscript in the British Museum dating from the time of Charles II (1660–85) illustrates a cornet very similar to the Bedford flag. The artist has labeled it "Thre County Trom," or Three County Troop. This was a cavalry company existing between 1659 and 1677 in Essex, Suffolk, and Middlesex counties in Massachusetts. It is quite possible that when that troop was disbanded, the flag was kept by the last cornet, that also being the title of the man who carried the flag. Bedford is in Middlesex County, and we know that Nathaniel Page's father and grandfather were cornets. So, long before the Revolution, this illustrious flag quite possibly flew in King Philip's War of 1675–76 and in other battles with the Indians. If this is true, the Bedford flag is roughly three hundred years old—the oldest banner preserved in the United States.

The Bedford flag is in very good condition, although the pole is missing. (The fringe is supposed to have been removed in the nineteenth century by a girl in the Page family and used to decorate a dancing gown.) Until its display in 1875, during the centennial celebration for the Battle of Concord, the flag was practically unknown, even around Bedford. Thus, Emerson probably did not realize that the flag he referred to still existed when he wrote this poem for the dedication of a monument in 1837 at the site of the battle:

> By the rude bridge that arched the flood,
> Their flag to April's breeze unfurled,
> Here once the embattled farmers stood
> And fired the shot heard round the world.

There is one earlier souvenir of the flag—a tombstone in the Bedford cemetery. At the top is a hand with a dagger, and below is the name of Charles Willson, captain of the Bedford minutemen. He was one of those who fell on the morning of April 19, 1775, faithful to the motto "Conquer or Die."

The colonists saw nothing strange in the fact that their flags were mostly British in design and meaning, and sometimes even British-made. They were, after all, British subjects living by the laws of Parliament under His Majesty's governors. The rights they so stoutly defended before the Revolution were the rights of free Englishmen, previously confirmed by the Magna Carta and the Glorious Revolution of 1689. So when the citizens of Taunton, Massachusetts, raised a liberty pole in the town common on October 21, 1774, it was the British Union Jack to which they added the words "Liberty & Union." Two years later Americans would have rejected the combination of that flag and that motto.

The Taunton flag, a modified Union Jack

LIBERTY AND UNION

Washington Takes Command

No one is ever really prepared for a revolution, not even the revolutionaries. And so it was in 1775. For a number of years the Americans had been protesting against British policies that they considered unjust. The colonists prospered on trade and found the Navigation Acts intolerable. They wanted land to develop and found themselves hemmed in by the Proclamation of 1763 that reserved western lands for the Indians. The pressure steadily increased later in the 1760's with the imposition of the Sugar Act, the Stamp Act, the Currency Act, the Quartering Act, and the Townshend Acts.

The colonists retaliated in various ways. Many laws were ignored; others were publicly challenged by prominent men. The Sons of Liberty and other radical groups rioted in the streets; on one occasion they wrecked the house of Thomas Hutchinson, the lieutenant governor of Massachusetts Bay. In 1770 British troops fired into a mob that had attacked them, killing five in the so-called Boston Massacre. In 1772 Rhode Islanders even burned British ships grounded off their coastline. And in 1773 "patriots" dressed as Indians boarded English ships in Boston harbor and dumped 342 chests of tea overboard. This was the famous Boston Tea Party to protest against the tax on tea that London had imposed. Men of good will on both sides worked to reconcile the growing differences, but events overtook them.

The skirmishes at Lexington and Concord in April, 1775, inflamed all the colonies. The Second Continental Congress met in Philadelphia the next month, illegally, to try to deal with the new stage of conflict. In many colonies regiments were formed under officers loyal to the American cause. In Boston itself the British commander, General Thomas Gage, began to fortify his position. In turn the rebel troops

General George Washington and his escort, the Philadelphia Light Horse, in 1775

established themselves on Breed's Hill in Charlestown, overlooking Boston. To drive them out, the British mounted an attack on June 17, 1775, in what came to be known as the Battle of Bunker Hill. Gage's men won only at the price of very heavy losses. Americans were elated by the ability of their farmer-soldiers to stand up to British regulars, but they realized that if they were to be successful in the future, they would need organization and training as well as enthusiasm and courage.

The Second Continental Congress had named George Washington supreme commander of the American forces. On June 23, 1775, he left Philadelphia with the Philadelphia Light Horse as his escort. This cavalry company, commanded by Captain Abraham Markoe, was out-fitted by its wealthy Philadelphia members in elegant European-style uniforms. The company's color, or flag, was well suited to an elite corps. The yellow silk, 34" x 40", was fringed and embroidered with silver bullion, and the central design was painted in oils and gilt. It has been asserted that this flag accompanied Washington and the Light Horse on their trip to New York that June, although there is no firm proof. Since it was made before September, 1775, it seems likely that Washington saw the flag sometime during the course of that year. If he did, its canton—thirteen blue and silver stripes—may have appealed to him as an appropriate symbol for the thirteen colonies.

Continuing on from New York, Washington reached Cambridge, Massachusetts, where he spent the winter organizing his men into a regular army. Lacking money, ammunition, and experienced officers, Washington did not feel ready to commit his men to battle until the following spring. He was a thorough commander, and he knew that the penalty for failure would be trial as a traitor to the Crown.

Busy as he was between July, 1775, and March, 1776, Washington found time to think about flags. In July he ordered 78½ yards of red bunting for flags and twenty-two cod lines to hoist them with. These plain red flags flew over Winter Hill and Prospect Hill in Somerville (then part of Charlestown) and could be seen by the British in Boston. Three months later Washington's military secretary, Militia Colonel Joseph Reed, wrote to the patriots who were fitting out ships: "Please fix upon some particular flag . . . and a signal by which our vessels may know one another. What do you think of a flag with a white ground, a tree in the middle, the motto, 'Appeal to Heaven' . . . We are fitting out two vessels at Plymouth, and when I next hear from you on this subject I will let them know the flag and signal, that we may distinguish our friends from our foes."

The floating batteries that sailed down the Charles River in October, 1775, to blockade Boston flew this pine-tree flag. And since Massachusetts provided a great number of ships for the Continental Congress, the flag was also a familiar sight on the high seas.

Crescents and Rattlesnakes

Outside New England the pine tree was not popular, but a few other colonies had their own symbols. In South Carolina a silver crescent was worn as a cap-badge by local troops. A blue flag with a single crescent was raised over Fort Johnson in Charleston harbor on September 13, 1775, by Colonel William Moultrie (pronounced MOO-tree).

A year later the same flag, with the word "Liberty" added, flew over Fort Moultrie on Sullivan's Island in Charleston harbor. This fort was re-named in honor of the colonel after his heroic defense of it in June, 1776. During the battle the fort was under constant British bombardment for almost twelve hours. One of the shots from a British ship struck down the liberty flag. Sergeant William Jasper, risking his life, ran along the top of the breastworks, jumped to the beach, and retrieved the banner. Then he attached it to a sponge stick, a pole used

The flag flown at Fort Moultrie in 1776

in cleaning cannon, and planted it again firmly on the bastion. For his bravery Jasper was offered the rank of lieutenant by the governor. But he was embarrassed by his illiteracy and turned the promotion down.

Jasper's unit, the Second South Carolina Regiment of Continental Line, was presented with two embroidered silk flags. During the Battle of Savannah in 1778, three lieutenants were shot while trying to protect these colors. As the British advanced, Jasper again attempted to save the regimental flags. This time he was killed, and the flags were carried off to England as battle trophies. These South Carolina colors are typical of their time. Each was roughly square and richly fringed. The background was blue, the same shade as the uniform of the troops over which it flew. In the center was a distinctive emblem—in this case, a palmetto tree. The number of the regiment was inscribed in the upper corner.

Other regimental colors combined British and American symbols. The flag of the Second New Hampshire Regiment, Continental Line, showed a gold sun in the center of a buff field. Around the sun were thirteen interlaced rings, each labeled with the name of a state. But in the canton was an emblem resembling the British Union Flag. The same canton appeared in the banner of Colonel John Procter's 52nd Battalion of Associators, from Pennsylvania. In the center was a rattlesnake and the motto "Don't Tread on Me."

The rattlesnake was the favorite animal emblem of the Americans even before the Revolution. In 1751 Benjamin Franklin's *Pennsylvania Gazette* carried a bitter article protesting the British practice of sending convicts to America. The author suggested that the colonists return the favor by shipping "a cargo of rattlesnakes, which could be distributed in St. James Park, Spring Garden, and other places of pleasure, and particularly in noblemen's gardens." Three years later the same paper printed the picture of a snake as a commentary on the Albany Congress. To remind the delegates of the danger of disunity, the serpent was shown cut into pieces. Each segment was marked with the name of a colony, and the motto "Join, or Die" appeared below. Other papers took up the snake theme.

This was Benjamin Franklin's warning against disunity among the colonies in 1754.

By 1774 the segments of the snake had grown together, and the motto (in the New York *Journal*) had been changed to read: "United Now Alive and Free Firm on this Basis Liberty Shall Stand and Thus Supported Ever Bless Our Land Till Time Becomes Eternity." The New York *Gazetteer* published a poem about these snake pictures:

> Ye Sons of Sedition, how comes it to pass
> That America's typ'd by a Snake—in the grass?
> Don't you think 'tis a scandalous, saucy reflection,
> That merits the soundest, severest Correction?

Other authors felt the rattlesnake was a good example of America's virtues. They argued that it is unique to America; individually its rattles produce no sound, but united they can be heard by all; and while it does not attack unless provoked, it is deadly to step upon one.

The rattlesnake emblem was especially popular in Rhode Island. At least three flags from that colony showed the snake coiled to strike and the warning motto "Don't Tread On Me." One, carried at the siege of Newport in 1778, had a field of blue and white stripes. Another.

the flag of the United Company of the Train of Artillery from Providence, showed the snake surrounded by thirteen stars, with the addition of the traditional Rhode Island anchor. Commodore Esek Hopkins flew a similar flag as the first commander in chief of the American Navy. Colonel Christopher Gadsden, a member of the Marine Committee of the Continental Congress, was so impressed by Hopkins' standard that he presented a copy of it to the legislature of his home state, South Carolina. (This is why it is sometimes mistakenly called the South Carolina, or Gadsden, flag.) Still another rattlesnake flag flown by many American ships during the Revolution, either as a jack or an ensign, had a background of red and white stripes.

Commodore Esek Hopkins' standard, 1776

Another naval rattlesnake flag of 1776

How the Regiments Got Their Colors

Many of the early American regimental flags were improvised on the spur of the moment, like the one made and raised at Fort Schuyler in August, 1777. In a journal kept by one of the soldiers we read: "the Fort had never been Supplyed with a Flagg. The importance of having one on the arrival of the Enemy had set our Injenuity to work, and a respectable one was formed. The white stripes where Cut out of Ammunition Shirts the blue strips out of the Cloak Formarly mentioned taken from the Enemy at Peeks-kill. The red stripes out of different pieces of Stuff Collected from sundry persons. The Flagg was sufficiently large and a general Exhilaration of Spirits appeared on beholding it Wave the Morning after the arrival of the Enemy."

Few regimental colors originated as romantically as the so-called Eutaw Flag carried by a cousin of George Washington, Colonel William Washington, during the Revolution. Traveling south from his native

A Boston newspaper illustration of 1780

Virginia to South Carolina at the head of a cavalry troop, he was warmly received by the Elliott family at their house, "Sandy Hill," west of Charleston. Before long, friendship deepened into love, and William became engaged to the Elliott's daughter, Jane. When it came time for him to leave, Jane assured him she would wait anxiously for news of every battle fought under his banner. William replied that she would wait in vain, for his company had no flag. Jane promptly made one. From a large piece of crimson damask—perhaps an elegant living-room curtain—she cut a piece about two feet square that she hemmed and fringed.

Bearing this flag, William Washington and his troops won a brilliant victory at the Battle of Cowpens on January 17, 1781. It was then carried in other battles, including the Battle of Eutaw Springs that gave the banner the name by which it is known today. After the Revolution William married Jane, and the flag was put away for forty-five years. Then, in 1827, the widowed Mrs. Washington gave the historic banner to the Washington Light Infantry Corps of Charleston, which displays it on very special occasions.

George Washington felt that an army without flags would lack spirit and discipline. As early as February, 1776, he issued an order requiring regimental colonels to confer about flags with their brigadiers and with the quartermaster general. They were to pick for the background a color associated with the regimental uniform "and such motto as the colonel may choose." There was to be a standard for the whole regiment and colors for each of the companies. One such flag made for the First Pennsylvania Regiment, Continental Line, was green. On a red center were a hunter and a tiger in white. The motto was "Domari Nolo" ("I Refuse to be Subjugated").

Two years later a list was compiled of regimental flags then in use. Out of the seventy-four reported, twenty-nine were in poor condition. In any event, Washington wanted to establish a new system of regimental flags. There were now to be two colors for every regiment, as in European armies. One of these would be a regimental standard; the other would be a new flag representing the United States, and it would be the same for all regiments. Only after much debate were the designs for the two banners decided upon and orders placed. Further delays were caused by the shortage of silk—which had to be imported from France. When the colors were finally ready, no one thought to tell Washington, who found them in a military storehouse in March, 1783. By then the war was over, and a year later the Continental Army was down to eighty men. The new flags were never used; history does not record what became of them, and we do not know even what they looked like.

II. THE GROWTH OF THE NATION AND ITS FLAG

The Continental Colors

January 1, 1776, dawned cold and windy in Boston. Lieutenant General Sir William Howe was short-tempered from having been encircled in the city for six months by the motley crowd of farmer-soldiers he had defeated at Bunker Hill. It was a stalemate: there weren't enough British to break out of Boston, yet they were sufficiently strong to keep the Americans from attacking.

Howe's reveries were interrupted by an aide who brought what seemed to be good news. British lookouts had been watching the rebel signal stations on Winter Hill and on Prospect Hill. Today, instead of the usual red flag of revolution, the Continentals had hoisted a large new flag on "Mount Pisga," as the British had nicknamed Prospect Hill. (This referred to the Biblical mountain from which Moses was allowed to view the Promised Land that he was not permitted to enter.)

The Continentals' new flag had the Union Flag in the canton and thirteen red and white stripes. Howe felt that it must be a sign of reconciliation with Britain. No doubt the king's speech to Parliament in October, 1775, had done the trick. The speech had warned the colonists of severe penalties for continuing to resist the lawful orders of His Majesty. When the copies of that speech had arrived in Boston, Howe had seen to it that some were sent to the Continentals. This new flag with the Union Flag in the canton must be their reply.

The situation across the Charles River was not quite as Howe imagined it. Washington had indeed sent word from his headquarters in Cambridge that a great union flag was to be raised on Prospect Hill. But surrender was the furthest thing from his mind: the flag was to be hoisted "in compliment to the United Colonies." In addition he ordered thirteen guns fired and a like number of cheers given. The occasion was the formal creation that day of the Continental Army. The king's speech, which would only infuriate the Americans when they read it, had not yet been received. A contemporary newspaper reports that the Continental soldiers, far from giving up their positions, were "all

A Broadway parade by New York's Seventh Regiment in the first year of the Civil War

Striped nautical flags were flown even in 1588, the year of the Spanish Armada.

in barracks, in good health and spirits . . . the whole army impatient for an opportunity of action."

How the Flag Got Its Stripes

The union flag on Prospect Hill apparently misled General Howe because it was a design he had never seen before. In 1775—indeed, until the Declaration of Independence the next year—Americans were theoretically Englishmen fighting for their traditional rights. Their emblem, therefore, did not symbolize separation from the mother country. Its stripes stood for unity among the thirteen colonies, but its canton indicated loyalty to the Crown. This flag, known as the Continental Colors, was never officially adopted, yet it continued to wave over American forts and ships until at least December, 1777.

Where did the stripes come from? They definitely did not come from Washington's coat of arms or from the rings on the tail of Mrs. Washington's tomcat, as some writers have suggested. While we are not certain of their actual source, there are several likely possibilities. In previous years, as we have seen, the British Red Ensign had been a very common sight in America. In at least three important cases—the Endecott, New England, and Taunton flags—it had been modified by the colonists. So it is quite possible that the Continental Colors were created simply by adding white stripes to the red field of the British merchant ensign. (It is probably only a coincidence that a striped flag of exactly the same design was already being flown in the Orient by the East India Company.) But even if this is true, it does not tell us why stripes were chosen.

One possible reason is the European tradition of flying striped nautical flags. Royal banners were not allowed on private ships, and complicated heraldic designs were hard to distinguish at a distance. So privately owned ships frequently flew as an ensign either the national flag or a striped flag using the two principal colors of the royal banner. Striped ensigns made up from the French royal banner were blue and white, Portuguese ones were green and white, Prussian ones black and white, and so on. English ships often flew red and white striped flags, with or without the cross of St. George (or the Union Flag) in the canton. The number of stripes usually made no difference. But of course in America the number thirteen had special meaning. So early American flags often had either thirteen stripes or twenty-seven—that is, thirteen red stripes on a white background.

Another possible source of the stripes is the flag of the Sons of Liberty. Before the Revolution these radicals met under "liberty poles" or "liberty trees" at the top of which a flag was often flown. The Sons of Liberty flag was composed of five red and four white stripes, with no canton or central emblem. Flags like this, but with thirteen stripes, were hoisted by American merchant ships in the early years of the war.

41

Whatever the source it is certain that stripes were a popular American symbol both before and during the Revolution.

A New Constellation

The Continental Colors, the first national flag of the United States, had a brief but glorious history. It flew from the flagship of the American fleet, the *Alfred*, on December 3, 1775, possibly raised by John Paul Jones. At St. Eustatius it received the first salute to the United States from a foreign power—the Netherlands. In 1777 the French saluted the Continental Colors flying over the sloop *General Mifflin* at Brest, France. When Continental troops captured New Providence in the Bahamas in March, 1776, the Colors became the first American flag to fly over a captured foreign fort. Although the Continental Colors was not used by the Army, it did fly over forts and public buildings.

The Continental Colors became obsolete long before it was replaced. The Declaration of Independence, in July, 1776, was a formal proclamation to the world that the United States had broken its ties with Britain. Yet Congress waited until June, 1777, before eliminating the Union Flag from the canton of the Continental Colors. There seem to have been many reasons for the delay. From the summer of 1776 to the next summer the Americans suffered a number of military reverses. Since the supply of ammunition and other war materiel was a grave problem, few people had time to think about changing flags.

The Continental Colors was widely used as an ensign, and at least one Navy man did become concerned about its continued use after the Declaration of Independence. As keeper of naval supplies in Philadelphia William Richards was responsible for outfitting vessels on the Delaware River. Like any good businessman, he didn't want to be stuck with obsolete goods. So in August, 1776, he wrote to the Pennsylvania Committee of Safety asking for the correct design of the naval flag. He repeated his request in October, but there is no record of anyone having answered his letters.

Others were interested in the flag for different reasons. In 1777 Thomas Green, an Indian, sent some wampum to the Continental Congress in Philadelphia and asked that they forward to him a United States flag. He explained that the chiefs of his tribe would carry it to guarantee their safety while traveling in American territory. Unfortunately, there is no record of the action Congress took.

George Washington, Betsy Ross, and the legendary creation of The Stars and Stripes

Finally, on June 14, 1777, Congress adopted the following brief resolution: "Resolved That the Flag of the united states be 13 stripes alternate red and white, that the Union be 13 stars white in a blue field representing a new constellation." This motion was inscribed in the journals of Congress without any discussion and without any picture of the flag. Apparently the founding fathers regarded it as a routine piece of business that required no comment. Historians have had many occasions since to regret their silence!

Betsy Ross and Francis Hopkinson

There are fascinating stories, some historical documents, and a great deal of speculation about how The Stars and Stripes was born, but we do not have the final answer today, and perhaps we never will. The Betsy Ross story relies on a romantic family tradition. Those who support Francis Hopkinson as the designer refer to historical documents, and some have traced the history of the flag's stars back sixteen hundred years.

In February, 1776, Washington had ordered each colonel to design a flag for his regiment. In May, while reviewing the troops in Philadelphia, he noted that many units still lacked standards, and he wrote the following reminder to Major General Israel Putnam, his commander in New York: "I desire you'll speak to the several Col^ls & hurry them to get their colours done."

Then legend takes over from history. Early in June Robert Morris and George Ross, both prominent Pennsylvania statesmen, discuss a new flag to replace the Continental Colors. Colonel Ross suggests to Washington that his nephew's widow, Mrs. John Ross, may be able to help. Young Betsy has already sewn shirt ruffles for Washington, and he readily agrees to seek her advice. When the three men arrive at Mrs. Ross's upholstery shop on Arch Street, they are shown into the back room. Washington asks Betsy if she can make up a copy of a new flag, and he shows her a sketch of the proposed design.

Looking at the rough sketch, Mrs. Ross says she is sure she can do the job. But, she asks, wouldn't it be better if the flag were a rectangle instead of a square? And instead of scattering the stars in the canton, wouldn't they look better arranged in a circle? Finally, wouldn't five-pointed stars be better than six-pointed ones? Washington nods his head in agreement, and as she talks he draws a new sketch with all the changes. A practical man, the general asks if five-pointed stars are easy to make. With a few quick folds and a single snip of her scissors, Betsy produces a perfect five-pointed star. The men are convinced and leave the shop.

Shortly afterward a messenger instructs Betsy Ross to visit a certain shipping company at the wharves. There a man gives her a water color of the flag as it is to be made. He also gives her some old flags so that she can see how they have been made, for Mrs. Ross has never sewn a flag before. When the big flag is finished, the committee decides it is the best of several patterns. So the flag is presented to Congress, which makes it official. Betsy Ross is given a government contract to make as many flags as she can. And so, aided by her daughters and other relatives, she continues for the next fifty years to make copies of the Stars and Stripes.

Is this tale true? We cannot say for sure, but the evidence is strongly against it. Would so important and busy a man as George Washington have taken an afternoon off to discuss the design of a flag? Would he have asked for, or accepted, the opinions of a woman who had never made a flag before? Why was the first design square when all other American naval flags were rectangular? Why was a new flag even being considered in May, 1776? We know that the Continental Colors, barely six months old, continued to fly for more than a year. And it is not likely that the new flag, with its obvious rejection of British symbols, would have been selected before the adoption of the Declaration of Independence. Moreover, there is no record in the congressional journals of June, 1776, that this flag was adopted. If the flag was made in Philadelphia, why did William Richards, the local naval-stores keeper, ask about the national flag in August and October of that year? Why don't we have any accounts of The Stars and Stripes in actual use until August, 1777? Even the story of the five-pointed star is unconvincing: many American flags, even years later, had stars with six points.

Finally, we know almost nothing about Mrs. Ross. There is a bill paid to her in May, 1777, for (unidentified) ships' colors, and there is a single portrait, discovered in 1963, but that is all. Her connection with the original Stars and Stripes is not mentioned in the writings of any contemporary. No newspaper or official document says a single word about the congressional committee, the sample flags made by other seamstresses, the adoption of a flag in 1776, or an order for more flags. The only evidence is the family story first told to the public by Mrs. Ross's grandson in 1870, almost a century after the event. This man said he had heard it at his grandmother's knee. But he was only eleven when his grandmother died at age eighty-four, and it is easy to imagine how the story could have become confused.

Even if Betsy Ross did sew the first flag, who made the sketch she followed? Here we have some contemporary evidence to help us. Three years after the flag was approved by Congress, the Board of Admiralty

OVERLEAF: *On inauguration day in 1789, Washington is rowed across New York harbor.*

45

received a letter from Francis Hopkinson, a poet, artist, designer of seals, member of the Continental Congress, treasurer of loans, judge, and chairman of the Continental Navy Board. In his letter he listed various things he had designed for the government and asked for some public wine as payment. He had, he wrote, "with great Readiness upon several Occasions exerted my small abilities in this Way for the public service, as I flatter myself, to the satisfaction of those I wished to please."

Among the designs he claims to have made, Hopkinson lists "the Flag of the United States of America." But Congress turned down his request for payment in wine. He was not the only person who had contributed to the designs for government flags and seals, they insisted.

What about the stars in the flag? Ever since the adoption of the flag in 1777 they have been a popular American symbol. A new star in the flag has announced to the nation and to the world that a new state has joined the Union. The star itself has become an international symbol of sovereignty and independence because of its use in the United States flag. Before 1777 the star symbol was very rare, but today sixty national banners display one or more stars.

It is not clear when the star first appeared in American heraldry. A Massachusetts coin of 1776 showed thirteen stars. In Rhode Island the military colors of the First and Second regiments each had thirteen stars, although we do not know when those flags were made. It is possible that the Rhode Island stars were copied from the seals of Providence and Portsmouth, which date to at least 1676. If this is true, then the line can be traced back even further. Portsmouth, Rhode Island, probably took its stars from the seal of Portsmouth, England. That city was granted a star and crescent as a badge in 1194 by King Richard I. Richard, in turn, had found the crescent and star in the Near East during the Crusades. The crescent was the ancient symbol of Diana, the patron goddess of Byzantium. When the emperor Constantine renamed Byzantium "Constantinople" in A.D. 330, he dedicated it to the Virgin Mary. Her emblem, the star, was added to Diana's crescent. If this genealogy of the American star is correct, it carries the history of the flag back sixteen hundred years.

The First Stars and Stripes

The law of 1777 and the flag itself became known very slowly. There is some reason to believe that the flag was flown in Philadelphia on July 4,

1777, the first anniversary of the Declaration of Independence. Ezra Stiles, later president of Yale, wrote about the new flag in his diary in July. The next month it was mentioned for the first time in a newspaper. But since in the eighteenth century flags were flown less frequently than they are today, even several years later the exact design of the flag was not very well known. Six years after its adoption the flag law was published in the *Pennsylvania Gazette* with a request that other newspapers copy it so that more people would know about the flag.

Actually, the design of the first flag was not at all standardized. Today, when hundreds of thousands of United States flags are manufactured every year for use by private citizens, businesses, the armed forces, and the government, every detail is carefully defined. The red and blue are matched to special shades and must be made with just the right dyes. The exact size and placement of each star and each stripe is set out in an Executive Order. Otherwise each manufacturer would create his own version of the flag.

That was the situation in 1777. Congress had not indicated how the stars of the "new constellation" were to be arranged. Usually they were in rows of three-two-three-two-three or four-five-four stars. Sometimes they were grouped in a rectangle or rough circle around the edge of the blue canton. In this case the thirteenth star was usually put in the center, as in the flag of the Third Maryland Regiment. (The version often illustrated today, with thirteen stars in a perfect circle, was almost unknown at the time the flag was used.) Sometimes the stars were arbitrarily scattered over the canton, as in the flag of Ethan Allen's Green Mountain Boys, who captured Fort Ticonderoga from the British. In the Bennington (Vermont) Flag of 1777 the stars have seven points—another common variation. The *Alliance* and Guilford Courthouse flags had stars with eight points. Others had four-, five-, or six-pointed stars, because the law was silent about this detail.

The most unexpected feature of many of the old flags is their stripes. The Bennington Flag has six red stripes on a white field, instead of the familiar seven red and six white stripes. In North Carolina there exists a strange flag with red and blue stripes; its stars are blue on a white canton. Yet this flag was probably made four years after the flag law of 1777! Even leading members of the government in that era did not know—or did not care—about the correct flag. In 1778 Benjamin Franklin and John Adams wrote to the king of Naples: "the flag of the United States of America consists of 13 stripes, alternately red, white and blue; a small square in the upper angle, next the flag staff,

The Green Mountain Boys and their flag   The Bennington, Vermont, banner

is a blue field with 13 white stars." At the Dutch island of Texel in
the North Sea John Paul Jones flew such a blue-red-white striped flag
on the captured British warship *Serapis* (pronounced se-RAPE-is). A
faithful picture of the flag, painted by someone who saw the ship on
October 5, 1779, was discovered in 1921.

    The first banner with thirteen stars and thirteen stripes known to
have flown in battle was the Bennington Flag, which is still preserved
in Vermont. It flew on August 16, 1777, in an American victory there
that paved the way for a further triumph a few months later at Sara-
toga. John Paul Jones claims the honor of obtaining the first salute to
the new flag at sea. On February 14, 1778, the French admiral La Motte
Picquet fired his cannon as a mark of respect for the American flag
flying on the *Ranger* at Quiberon Bay. The *Columbia*, a merchant ship
from Boston, first carried The Stars and Stripes around the world in its
voyage of 1787–90.

    The same flag that witnessed American victory in the Revolution
and the hardships of the young nation continued to be used until 1795.
By then it was recognized by the European powers as the banner of a
free nation.

The Star-Spangled Banner

During the Revolution Vermont was not represented in Congress. In
fact, until 1791 it was not a state at all, but an independent republic.

The flag flown by the captured Serapis   *The Battle of Guilford Courthouse Flag*

Once its land disputes with New Hampshire and New York were settled, Vermont became the fourteenth state. The following year, 1792, Kentucky became the first of the "western" states to join the original thirteen that bordered the East Coast. At first these two new states were not represented in the national standard.

In December, 1793, Senator Stephen R. Bradley of Vermont proposed a new flag law. The brief text, which simply added two stars and two stripes to the existing flag, was quickly passed and sent on to the House of Representatives. There it met considerable opposition, especially from Benjamin Goodhue of Massachusetts. He could not imagine that the Senate had nothing better to do with its time than to pass on such trivial matters. Moreover, he complained, a flag should be permanent. If a new star and a new stripe were added for every state, the country might eventually find itself flying a banner with as many as twenty stars and twenty stripes. Representative Israel Smith of Vermont, ignoring the honor involved for his home state, pointed out the cost involved: every shipowner in the nation would have to pay at least sixty dollars to change his flags.

Despite the opposition, the bill was approved by a narrow margin, and the fifteen-star, fifteen-stripe flag became official on May 1, 1795. During the twenty-three years it was used, it became the first United States flag to be raised in victory over a fort in the Old World. This occurred during an unofficial war with the Barbary Coast states of North Africa when on April 27, 1805, on "the shores of Tripoli" of the Marine Corps hymn, the fort at Derna fell to the Americans.

Francis Scott Key gazes at The Star-Spangled Banner flying over Fort McHenry in 1814.

The second official American flag is also The Star-Spangled Banner of the national anthem, immortalized by Francis Scott Key in 1814. The United States was at war with Britain, and on the night of September 13–14 the British were attempting to destroy Fort McHenry outside Baltimore. Key, a young Washington lawyer, and a friend were being held by the British aboard a ship in the harbor. The British poured cannon and rocket fire into the fort all night long. But the next morning the Americans saluted The Star-Spangled Banner, which still waved triumphantly over the unvanquished fort.

Key was so moved that he penned a poem, which was published in a number of newspapers and very soon was sung in public to the tune of "To Anacreon in Heaven." This had been a drinking song in England, but in America it was the tune for about twenty different patriotic lyrics. Over the years Key's words became very popular, and finally, in 1931, "The Star-Spangled Banner" was selected as the official national anthem. The Fort McHenry flag is preserved, although it has lost many pieces in battle—and to souvenir hunters. It now forms the central exhibit in the newest building of the Smithsonian Institution in Washington, D.C.

The Nation Moves Forward

On December 11, 1816, Indiana entered the Union as its nineteenth state. The troublesome question of the flag, foreseen by Representative Goodhue a quarter-century before, had arisen again. Officially, nothing had been done to represent Tennessee, Ohio, and Louisiana in the flag. In fact, all kinds of flags were flying, with anything from thirteen stars and thirteen stripes to nineteen stars and nineteen stripes.

On the day of Indiana's entry into the Union, Representative Peter H. Wendover of New York proposed that a committee be set up to look into the question of a new flag. Wendover himself was appointed chairman. The committee promptly reported back to Congress that it was sure the American people wanted no radical change in their flag, but that they would like to see new states represented. The idea—approved in 1794—of adding stripes as well as stars was not good, since it meant reducing the width of each stripe to maintain a given size flag. So the committee recommended a return once and for all to the original number of stripes, thirteen. On the other hand the committee felt that a star should be added to signal the entry of each new state, on the July 4th following that state's admission to the Union.

Wendover's brilliant idea not only brought the flag up to date with twenty stars (another state had joined by the time the law went into effect); it automatically provided for the twenty-four changes that have been made in the flag since 1818. Although the arrangement of the stars was not given in this law, the government began to issue specifications. Gradually these official patterns replaced designs made according to personal whim. Throughout the nineteenth century, however, it was common to see fanciful forms of the flag. One of the most popular designs showed the stars surrounding the coat of arms of the United States. At other times the stars were arranged in the form of a large star, a circle, or some other geometric form. One unusual variation was carried by the Western explorer John C. Frémont, who later became the first Republican candidate for President of the United States. Between the rows of stars in the canton of his flag was an eagle. The eagle held the usual arrows of war, but the olive branch of peace was replaced by the calumet, or peace pipe. Frémont hoped that this would be accepted by the Indians he met in his travels as a token of his peaceful intentions.

Each of the twenty-seven official flags of the United States has witnessed some significant event in the growth of the nation. During the Civil War President Lincoln refused to omit the stars that stood for the states in rebellion. In fact, the war began with a flag of thirty-three stars and ended with one of thirty-five—the new stars for Kansas and West Virginia. (Many of the flags carried by Union troops had gold instead of white stars.) The flag with thirty-seven stars flew at

In the 1840's John C. Frémont carried this flag while exploring the Far West.

54

Promontory Summit in Utah in 1869 when the nation was linked by the first transcontinental railroad. Two years earlier a banner with the same number of stars was the first American flag to fly over the new territory of Alaska.

The Spanish-American War carried the forty-five star flag to the Caribbean and the Philippines, and the forty-eight star flag went to Europe in 1917 during World War I. A little more than twenty years later this same flag returned to Europe and traveled to Asia during United States participation in World War II. The flag of forty-eight stars lasted from 1912 to 1959—longer than any other pattern. It was replaced by the forty-nine-star flag, to include Alaska. The present design of fifty stars signaled the entry of Hawaii into the Union in 1959. Today the diplomatic, commercial, and military interests of the nation are worldwide: there is scarcely any nation where The Star-Spangled Banner cannot be found displayed somewhere. It has been planted by courageous men at both poles, on the highest mountains, at the bottom of the sea. It has been carried to the moon; perhaps before the end of the century it will fly on another planet.

The first transcontinental railroad was completed at Promontory Summit, Utah.

| Commodore Oliver Hazard Perry's flag | The banner that flew over the Alamo |

America's Other Flags

In all its successes and all its defeats The Stars and Stripes has not been alone. The rich flowering of banners during the Revolution proved to be only a beginning. Ever since, Americans have created new flags of all kinds—patriotic, military, personal; for their businesses, their organizations, their political groups; to distinguish government offices, states and cities, shipping companies, and scout troops.

Flags have long spoken of the willingness of Americans to defend their ideals. During the Revolution we chose defiant mottoes like "Liberty and Union," "Don't Tread on Me," and "Conquer Or Die." Such words did not disappear once independence was won. In the War of 1812, for example, as Captain James Lawrence of the *Chesapeake* died, his last order was "Don't give up the ship!" Commodore Oliver Hazard Perry made this his battle cry the following year when he fought the British in the Battle of Lake Erie. It was emblazoned in bold letters on a blue banner that flew from his flagship, the *Lawrence*. American settlers in Texas found themselves oppressed by the Mexican dictator Santa Anna in the 1830's. At first their response was mild: they flew a Mexican flag bearing the date of the old, liberal constitution (1824). Soon, however, the Texans unfurled banners with mottoes like "Our Country's Rights or Death." And when Texas finally became an independent republic, it chose a lone-star flag that resembled the American ensign.

Southerners in the nineteenth century used many different flags to express their opposition to policies they felt the North was imposing upon them. They waved "the Bonnie Blue Flag that bears a single star" and revived the crescent-flag of South Carolina. When the Confederate government first met in February, 1861, one of its initial acts was to create a flag committee. The next month this group proposed, but did not adopt, the famous "Stars and Bars" as a national flag. Like the flag of Texas, it was obviously patterned after The Stars and Stripes. The bars were red, white, and red, and the canton had white stars for each state. (At first there were seven states, but the Confederacy soon recognized six more members.)

In the Battle of Bull Run the flags of the opposing forces looked so much alike that each side accused the other of using its flag as a trick. Several Confederate generals got together and decided to make a special battle-flag that would differ both from the Stars and Bars and The Stars and Stripes. It was made square so that it could be carried on horseback. Its red background could easily be seen at a distance, and its narrow white border reinforced the edges against ripping. The thirteen white stars were set on a blue saltire, or diagonal cross. This

The Confederate Battle Flag led southern troops into combat at Gettysburg in 1863.

flag became very popular, although it was never made official.

In 1863 the Confederate Congress adopted an official national flag—one very different from the United States flag. It was a long oblong white flag with the Battle Flag in the canton. Two years later, at the very close of the war, a vertical red stripe was added at the end to keep the flag from looking like a flag of truce. But by then flags of truce were flying all over the Confederacy.

Reunited once again, Americans moved forward under The Stars and Stripes. Over the years the number of stars have kept pace with the growth of the nation. New flags have come and gone, as in the past, but the national flag has been the chief symbol of loyalty for Americans for more than a century. During Custer's Last Stand, at San Juan Hill, in the Ardennes, on the hill at Iwo Jima—the "broad stripes and bright stars" have served as a rallying point and a promise for the future.

Marines raise the American flag over Iwo Jima in March, 1945.

Tammany Hall in New York is festooned for the Democratic convention of 1868.

The Flag Today

In the past Americans treated the flag casually, despite their pride in it. It has appeared on pillowcases, rugs, curtains, chinaware, and furniture. The flag was draped on buildings and on speakers' platforms; from trees, and over horses and automobiles. In parades large flags were often carried flat by dozens of people who held the edges. Small flags decorated hats, blouses, and scarves. Schoolchildren, dressed in red, white, and blue, formed "living flags." During World War I instructions were devised for knitting little flags to send to soldiers.

In 1923 a flag code was written in Washington. Most of its provisions were simply common sense: the flag, as the chief symbol of the nation, should be treated with respect. During World War II this code was adopted by Congress, although no penalties were imposed on per-

On July 20, 1969, Neil A. Armstrong, commander of the Apollo 11 mission, and Colonel Edwin E. Aldrin, Jr., planted the American flag on the surface of the moon.

sons who did not follow the rules. In the 1960's the flag became the focus of many political disputes. Leftist groups often tore down and burned the flag as a symbol of American racism and imperialism. Others flew revolutionary flags such as the thirteen-star United States flag and the rattlesnake banner with the words "Don't Tread on Me." Segregationists in the South refused to fly The Stars and Stripes, even on public buildings. Instead they raised a modified version of the Confederate Battle Flag. Veterans' and patriotic groups convinced Congress that there should be a $1,000 fine and/or a year in jail for anyone convicted of desecrating the flag.

Americans have also become very interested in the history of their nation's flags. Tourists flock to see the original Revolutionary and Civil War flags still preserved around the country. Replicas of the famous banners of two hundred years ago fly again in museums and outdoor displays, in books and articles, in schools and color-guard groups. In Pittsburgh, for example, thirty-one historic flags are dramatically displayed at the Flag Plaza Foundation. And in Lexington, Massachusetts, where the first shots of the Revolution were fired, the Flag Research Center collects and publishes information on all kinds of American flags and symbols. Although many priceless flags have long been lost, efforts are being made to find and preserve those that remain. In the process, vexillologists (flag historians) have discovered long-forgotten facts about the origins of The Stars and Stripes.

The Vikings in Vinland. The Pilgrims at Plymouth. The Spanish in Florida. The Russians in California. The French at Fort Duquesne. John Endecott living according to his religious convictions. The Three County Troop battling the Indians. The Albany Congress and the first feeble attempts at unifying the colonies. The rebellious stripes of the Sons of Liberty. "Liberty" at Charleston; "Liberty and Union" at Taunton. The defiant arm and sword at Concord Bridge. The great union flag and stripes witnessing the birth of the American Army on Prospect Hill. The pine tree, the rattlesnake, and finally thirteen white stars "representing a new constellation." Then two more stripes and two more stars—The Star-Spangled Banner. A young nation growing, adding new states to the Union and more stars to its flag. The horrors of a Civil War, a new banner defying the old, then reconciliation. And finally, a mature nation taking its place in the world, facing its problems with courage, and aiming for the stars. This is America's heritage of flags.

2284-46-14
52
1/78